Space Technology
Space Tools
by Julie Murray
Dash!
LEVELED READERS
An Imprint of Abdo Zoom • abdobooks.com
3

Level 1 – Beginning
Short and simple sentences with familiar words or patterns for children who are beginning to understand how letters and sounds go together.

Level 2 – Emerging
Longer words and sentences with more complex language patterns for readers who are practicing common words and letter sounds.

Level 3 – Transitional
More developed language and vocabulary for readers who are becoming more independent.

THIS BOOK CONTAINS RECYCLED MATERIALS

abdobooks.com

Published by Abdo Zoom, a division of ABDO, PO Box 398166, Minneapolis, Minnesota 55439.
Copyright © 2020 by Abdo Consulting Group, Inc. International copyrights reserved in all countries.
No part of this book may be reproduced in any form without written permission from the publisher.
Dash!™ is a trademark and logo of Abdo Zoom.

Printed in the United States of America, North Mankato, Minnesota.
102019
012020

Photo Credits: Alamy, iStock, NASA
Production Contributors: Kenny Abdo, Jennie Forsberg, Grace Hansen, John Hansen
Design Contributors: Dorothy Toth, Neil Klinepier, Victoria Bates

Library of Congress Control Number: 2019941337

Publisher's Cataloging in Publication Data

Names: Murray, Julie, author.
Title: Space tools / by Julie Murray
Description: Minneapolis, Minnesota : Abdo Zoom, 2020 | Series: Space technology | Includes online resources and index.
Identifiers: ISBN 9781532129308 (lib. bdg.) | ISBN 9781098220280 (ebook) | ISBN 9781098220778 (Read-to-Me ebook)
Subjects: LCSH: Space tools--Juvenile literature. | Tools--Juvenile literature. | Space sciences--Juvenile literature. | Technology--Juvenile literature. | Astronautics--Juvenile literature.
Classification: DDC 629.4--dc23

Table of Contents

Space Tools

Space tools are items used in space. Space tools can be the special gear astronauts wear or the instruments they use.

Gear Used in Space

An astronaut wears a spacesuit while working outside of a spacecraft. It is called an extravehicular mobility unit (EMU).

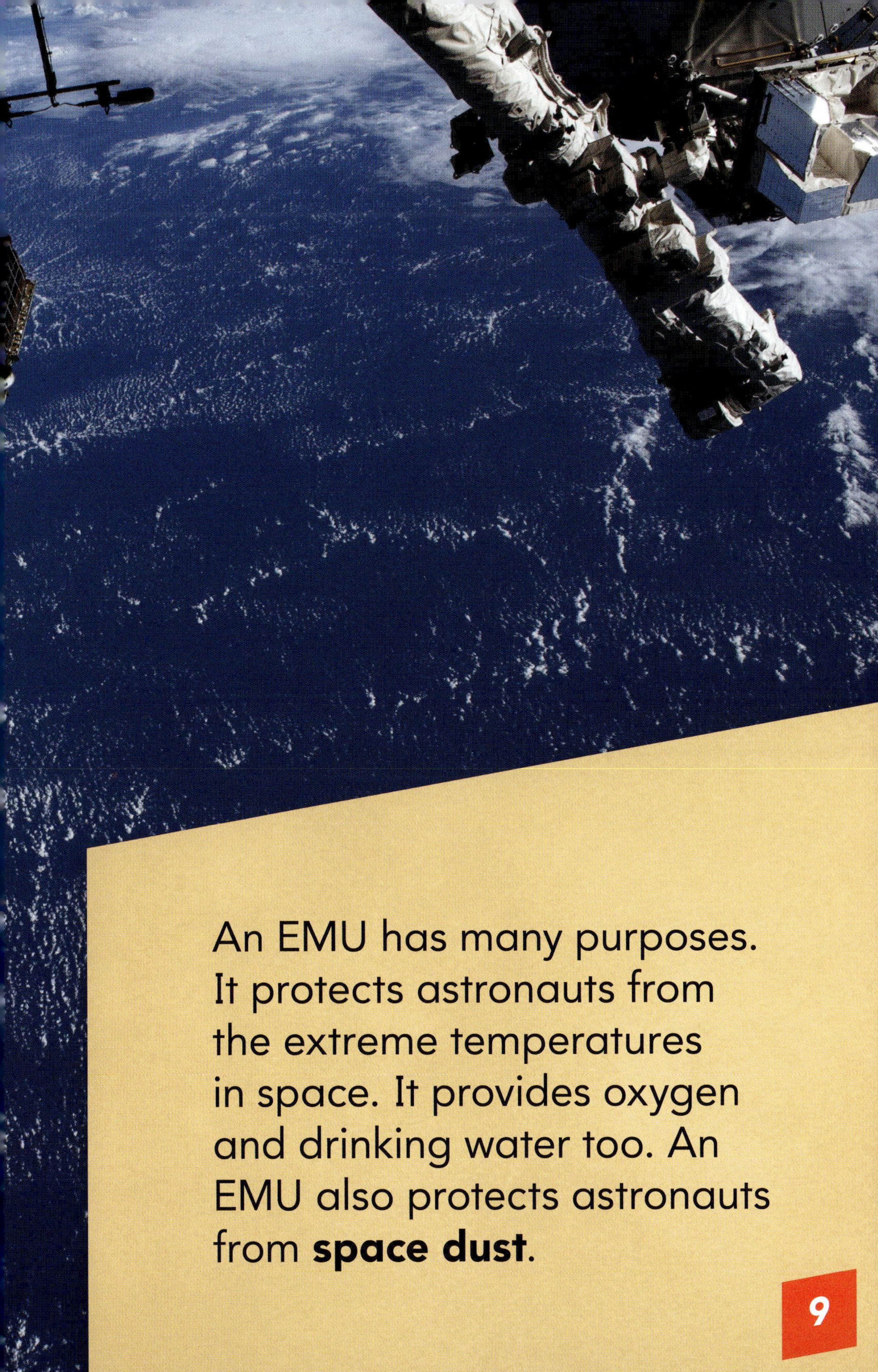

An EMU has many purposes. It protects astronauts from the extreme temperatures in space. It provides oxygen and drinking water too. An EMU also protects astronauts from **space dust**.

A helmet is worn over the head. It has lights and a camera. A hard piece is worn over the chest. This has the controls in it. The arms connect to the chest piece. Gloves are worn to protect the hands.

The lower part of the suit goes over the legs. Boots protect the feet. A special backpack is worn. It holds oxygen and provides electricity to the suit.

Tools Used
in Space

Astronauts use many different tools in space. NASA's pistol-grip tool is a cordless power drill. It helped build the **International Space Station (ISS)** and the Hubble Space Telescope.

A robot crane is like a long arm. The Canadarm2 is part of the **ISS**. It can move heavy objects. It also helps dock a space shuttle at the ISS. It can be controlled from the ground or inside the ISS.

Safety tethers keep items and astronauts safe in space. They are used to attach tools to the astronaut. Otherwise, the tools would float away. They also keep the astronaut attached to the spacecraft. The tethers help to control their movements and **stabilize** them.

All space tools are an important part of a space mission. They allow astronauts to perform **maintenance**, and repair or assemble equipment when needed. They also keep the astronauts safe!

NASA

- An EMU is white in color. White reflects the sun's heat. It can be more than 275 degrees Fahrenheit (135 degrees Celsius) in the direct sunlight.

- Astronauts wear a special device on their backs during space walks. It has small jets. This allows them to fly back to the spacecraft if their tether breaks.

- An EMU is big and heavy. It weighs about 300 pounds (136 kg). But it weighs nothing in space!

Glossary

International Space Station (ISS) – a large spacecraft in orbit around Earth. It serves as a home and science laboratory where crews of astronauts live and work. Several nations worked together to build it.

maintenance – work done to keep something working and in good condition.

space dust – also called cosmic dust, very fine particles of solid matter found in any part of the universe.

stabilize – to make steady.

Index

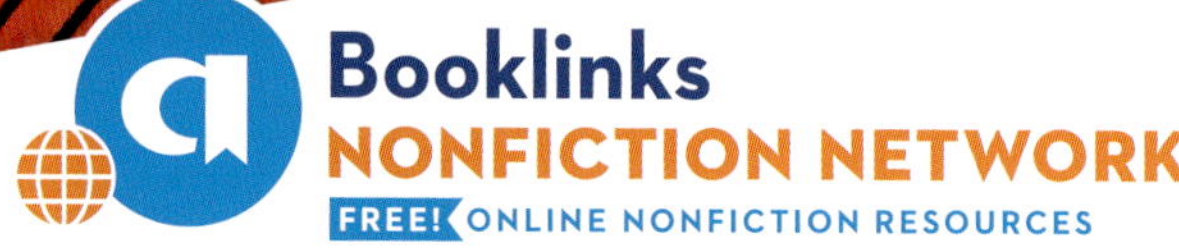

Online Resources

Booklinks
NONFICTION NETWORK
FREE! ONLINE NONFICTION RESOURCES

To learn more about space tools, please visit **abdobooklinks.com** or scan this QR code. These links are routinely monitored and updated to provide the most current information available.